The Adventures of Scuba Jack
Copyright 2020 by Beth Costanzo
All rights reserved

Koalas are one of Australia's best-known native animals! Koalas are commonly called Koala bears.

Koalas are marsupials. A marsupial is a mammal and has a pouch for its baby to live and grow. A baby koala is called a joey and it is born only 2 centimeters long. A joey lives in its mother's pouch for six months after birth. When a joey is born it is blind and has no ears, so it uses its strong sense of smell, touch, and instinct to find its way. Once a joey is strong enough, it will ride on its mother's back for another six months. Koalas grow to become big eaters! They pick the most nutritious and tastiest eucalyptus leaves from the trees. Koalas get their name from a term meaning "no drink" because they get almost all their moisture from the leaves and rarely drink water. Eucalyptus leaves are extremely tough and poisonous! Koalas have a cecum, which is a long digestive organ that allows them to break down the leaves unharmed.

Koalas have grey fur with a cream-colored chest, and they have very sharp claws to help them climb high into the trees. Koalas are around 2 feet tall and weigh 20 pounds. Did you know that Koalas have similar fingerprints to humans? Koalas are nocturnal which means they are mostly active at night.

Koalas do not have a lot of energy and sleep 18 to 22 hours a day. Koalas live up to 20 years in the wild.

Koalas Activities

Trace then rewrite the phrase below.

Count the koalas then circle the answer.

6   7   5

6   8   7

9   7   8

8   7   9

Koala Maze

Help the baby koala to find the plant

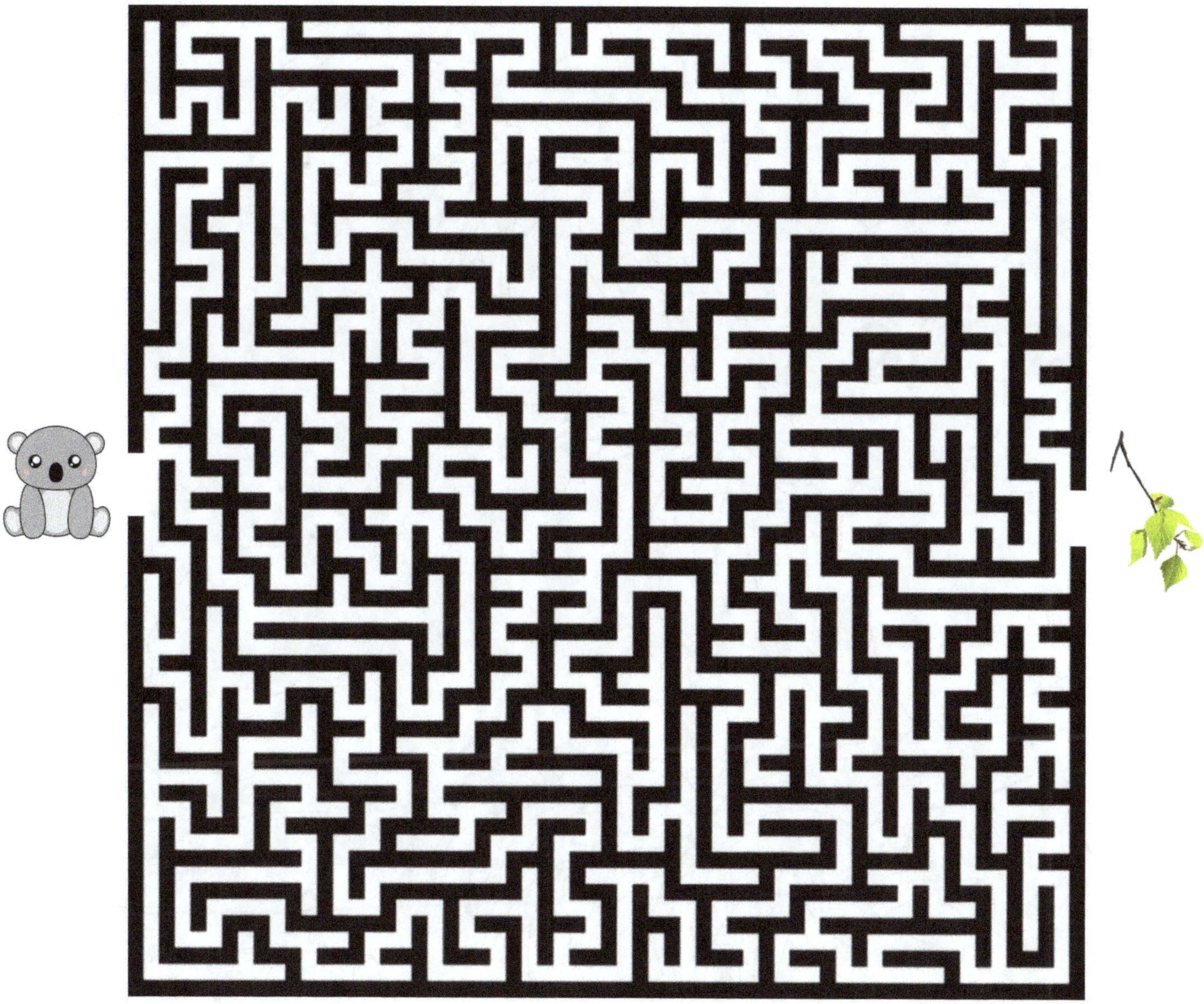

Koala Craft

1- Cut out the Koala Parts
2- Glue the ears to the back of the head
3- Glue the head to the body
4- Glue the paws to the bottom of the body

More Activities!

TRACE AND WRITE THE MISSING NUMBERS

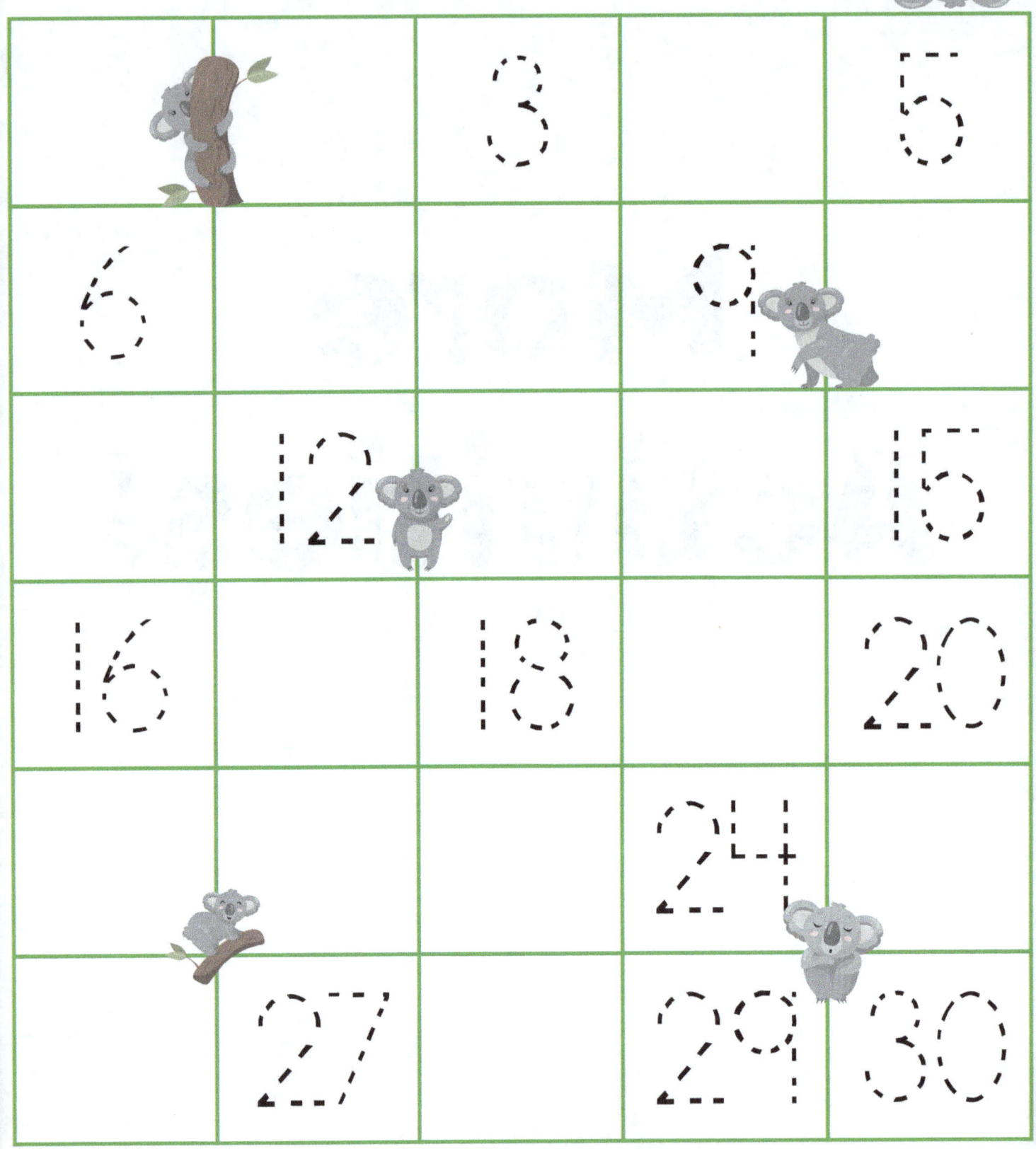

BABY ANIMAL

A baby Koala is called a joey

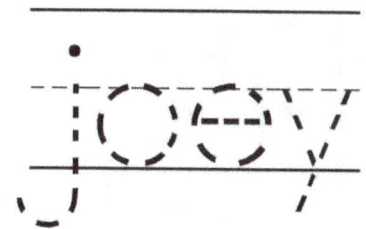

Count and write the number of joey below.

Color the Koala Bear

WORD SEARCH

Find and circle the words listed below.

J	O	E	Y	I	N	D	U	S	P
T	U	I	E	T	O	E	R	N	R
K	M	D	A	W	C	R	O	A	E
D	A	R	V	Y	T	E	A	I	A
O	N	M	E	C	U	L	A	L	R
R	R	O	S	R	R	U	P	S	S
C	W	C	B	A	N	A	S	K	A
C	L	A	W	S	A	E	I	L	A
S	V	O	C	T	L	P	U	S	H
E	U	C	A	L	Y	P	T	U	S

Joey   Eucalyptus   Claws   Blind

~~Ears~~   Nocturnal   Leaves

HELP KOALA TO FIND HER BABY

COLOR IT

Visit us at:

www.adventuresofscubajack.com